Untethered Love

BOBBIE ISABEL

Copyright © 2024
All rights reserved.
ISBN-13: 978-1-961045-10-1

For those who allow me to love them in the best way I know how until I learn better:

My children

My nugget

My person

Myself

A Note from the Poet

When I first started writing poetry, it served as a sort of therapy, allowing me to get out my emotions and work through my frustrations. Putting together my first collection, When Can We Be Soft?: Poems of Female Resistance helped me put so many of those frustrations into context. Sharing that book with the world was freeing and allowed me to write many of the poems you will find in this collection.

Untethered Love is about exploring the the types of love we can develop and express genuinely when we're free of the shackles society puts on us:

Part 1: For the Love of Nature: These poems are the manifestation of the adage "Stop and smell the roses." It is very hard to appreciate the splendor of nature when we're tied to past hurts.

Part 2: For the Love of a Child: While a child's love may be pure, it is difficult to reciprocate that same expression when responsibility weighs on us. Once the blinders of responsibility are removed, we can love unconditionally and with abandon.

Part 3: For the Love of Intimacy: Sex is easy. Physical intimacy does not necessarily require true connection, but it is so much better when we can be willing and fulfilled participants.

Part 4: For the Lost Promise of Love: Heartache and separation are a natural part of life. They are harder to endure when society tells us we are less than for not pushing through. Once that pressure is removed, we can appreciate the moments that were had and the positive impact they had on our lives.

Part 5: For the Love of Romance: When our hands are tied with societal and familial pressures, we often imagine love and romance where there is only lust and manipulation. Without those expectations, we are free to embrace authentic connection without fear and avarice.

Part 6: For the Love of Self: We start to learn at a young age all the reasons we should find ourselves lacking and all the ways we need to improve to make ourselves enticing to others. It isn't until we stop looking for others to evaluate our worth that we can begin to love ourselves completely.

I would love to say that there is a hierarchy for each type of love, but there's not. Some are more easily achieved, even existing when the rope is still knotted. Sometimes, we pick up the tethers and strap ourselves down again. And sometimes, as is the case with Self Love, we will forever be a work in progress. I hope that my journey of love resonates and you find yourself somewhere in these pages.

With all my love, Bobbie

Part I

FOR THE LOVE OF NATURE

April Morning

---

sunny april morn

perfect blossoms triumphant—

summer is coming

Wishes on the Wind

Wishes on the wind

Like Dandelions in the yard

Potential secured within a fingertip pod

The essence needed for rebirth

New beginnings haloed in moonlight

From the right angle swaddled

Hopes placed in toddler hands

For a moment's breath they fly free to the sun

Starling Murmurs

---

morning professions—
loving words beautiful as
starlings murmuring

Twitterpated

---

squeaks and squawks outside our window

twittering flaps of adolescent wings

spring arrives on Azalea petals

bright and bold when the heralds sing

hostas stretch to greet the sun

forward bend yoga poses

gentle bees bathed in green

frollicking amidst the roses

cuddled closely with ears attuned

gentle breezes rustling leaves

breaths synched with the Earth's renewal

basking in the spell Persephone weaves

Summer Call

---

cabin fever ache

like butterfly cocoon sleep—

summer's sun calls me

Guiding Constellations

When I am weary

I long for the comfort of home,

The security of place

And persons and pets.

Pyxis, guide my steps

Whether on Centaur's back

Or Pegasus's wing

I wander beneath

The distant stars

Searching for a different view

In a world indifferent

To my tempered steps

The gods look down

At my impermanence

With mocking disregard

Of their own extinction

I look to the sky

But not in prayer

I find Orion

And know that I am home

Spring Coming

---

clear sky, cool morning

lazy stroll along the beach

promise of warm days

Mother Ocean

Drowning in seas of emotion,

I come to you.

Your waves wash over me

Gently lapping at the sand

Between my toes,

Your energy soothes me.

Wading into the depths,

Your vastness caresses me.

The roar of your voice

Brings peace to my soul.

Even the face of your rage,

Wind howling

Water churning

Sand eroding

Your strength reinforces me.

In your presence,

I am renewed.

Owl in Flight

---

majestic wingspan

flutters in brown, white, and gold

great horned owl takes flight

Part II

FOR THE LOVE OF A CHILD

Disco Dilemma

Hit that baseline

Feel the claps

See him 'cross the room

Lifted shoes, the taps

Shaking in your boots

Skirt flowy swinging

Cheryl Lynn singing

It's got to be real

Can't stay away

Need your fix

Hoping the DJ

Will hit that funky mix

I want your love,

Now freak,

Waiting each day

For the end of the week

Trumpets blare

Boogie Wonderland

You step closer

Take his hand

Motions set

As you hustle

Night turning day

Polyester rustle

That's the way, uh huh

I like it.

Base drums play

Love to love you baby.

Do the deed

So much fun

Til the month just can't hide

And you can't run

Percussion playing in your ear

Telling him all your fear

That rock, skate, roll

Took love's toll

But he loved the nightlife

Action all he had to give

So he denied his part

And hardened your heart

A new heartbeat's rhythm

Built a new love true

You kept on dancing

Nine months through

Rooted and Buoyant

Rooted in depths of blue water

Buoyant in your radiance

We float at your whim

Hovering protectively

Watching you reign

And giving you reins

Over our hearts

As you grow

Surrounded

By love

Tiny Tornado

---

tiny tornado

leaving happy memories

all over the house

An Aunt's Perspective

He has

Toddler energy

An impish grin

and

A heart of gold

He tries

Pushing limits

New things

and

Patience

He gives

Profound love

Determination

and

Unending laughter

He needs

Understanding

Open space

and

Boundaries

Winsome Presence

Your cherubin smile

Brings peace to an otherwise anxious soul.

Your questioning eyes

Peer beyond the clouds of hidden pain.

Your exploring hands

Fingerpaint love in tiny gestures.

Your bouncy curls

Tendril around a guarded heart.

Your winsome presence

Is happiness personified.

Bubbles

iridescent spheres

cast against a gray sky

sprinkled with raindrops–

floating along a dreamscape,

childhood exists

in the fringes

of soap bubbles–

squeals of laughter

hidden amongst

groans of responsibility...

until magical wands wave

freedom for joy

Serenity

Precious moments in your presence **grant**

Permission of reconciliation within **me**

Promises that a new beginning brings **the**

Possibility of **serenity**

Through your eyes the ability **to**

Trust in a way I could never **accept**

Triumphantly pushing beyond **the**

Turbulence of tumultuous **things**

Of nightmares where **I**

Operated in response to what I **cannot**

Obtain until you brought peaceful **change**

Empty Nest

Tearful goodbyes

as they take their next steps

so different from the first ones

Toddling toward me

Arms outstretched

Not running away

Hands full of potential

Memories of bouncy energy

and high-pitched squeals

Joy and laughter fill my mind

Crowding out moments

of turned backs

and closed doors

Silence pervasive

House settling creaks

echoing through empty halls

Rooms dark

dusty with disuse

Dining table lonely

conversations with myself

Fridge laden with leftovers

from meals for three turned one

Love Letter from Mom

---

words can't describe the

profundity of my joy—

love letter from mom

Part III

FOR THE LOVE OF INTIMACY

Passion

Passion is not simply

A pattern of warm breath

On bare skin.

Passion exists where the

Oohs and aahs end.

Where bodies fail

But hearts beat

The silent cadence of

Knowing unchanged by time.

Passion is where the physical

And metaphysical intertwine

In shared DNA of being.

Your Scent

Bliss is

Wearing

Your shirt

Basking

In your scent

Pizzicato

---

hands slowly slide up

as arms encircle my waist

pulse quickening fast

your fingers

on my skin

pluck pizzicato

heartbeat tuned

Rambling

You apologize

for rambling,

I'm caught

on your

lips.

Dulcet tones in verse,

captivating melodies,

your voice calls to me.

Your voice sings to me

on a timpani of anticipation.

Breathy whispers on my skin,

it's timbre an embrace

within which I forget the world

and fold myself in its melody.

Kiss Me

---

as I watched his mouth

I bit my bottom lip hard—

thoughts of his kisses...

when he'd kissed my lips,

I sprang alive in hushed tones—

the heat in my cheeks

Longing

I long to manifest in your daydreams
The subtle curvature of your spine
Entangled in the web of my fingers
As you murmur a million promises

I long to sing the echoes of ecstasy
Conducting melodies of aspirations
To the gentle rumblings of aftershocks
While your smile rings triumphant salute

I long to enter apertures of trust
Laying aside the weight of vacillations
Gambling on cards not yet dealt
That your ante draws aces from fissures

I long to ride the waves of reality

Beckoning your presence from memories

Foretold in plots twisting to evolve

In our minds like complementary characters

I long to attain the wisdom of willows

Sheltering the shadows of hope

Still visible in the twinkle of starlight

Long after we explode into constellations

Sweet Release

bending my body

ensnaring all my senses

crashing sweet release

Part IV

FOR THE LOST PROMISE OF LOVE

Bathing Shadows

---

shadows of our forgotten

relationship

bathed

in

blue

light

Adrift

Your absence

Sets my heart

Adrift looking

For anchor

Hoja en Blanco

A blank page of longing

Where poetry should be

The inkwell long run dry

My love like a song

Surrendered to you

In a silent finality

Of unrequitedness

Love's Hill

Arguments aside

Love is the hill

I'll live

Upon

Withering Doubt

Doubt hangs in the balance,

threatening to snap

the tiny tethers of my resolve

as I try to adapt

to something beyond scraps

of burgeoning affection.

Intangible targets

hover in my periphery,

a siren song of anxiety

as I stare into your eyes,

praying that you'll quiet

the cacophony.

And then you hug me

until doubt withers away.

Touch Me...Again

I miss your fingers

the way they played on my neck

smooth legato

A Random Horse

Love, much like inspiration,
develops from unlikely encounters.
A chance coffee shop meeting,
or perhaps a dog park rendezvous.
Much like finding a random horse
frolicking in an empty field
No history or future concerns
beyond the here and now,
living in the present
creating art from that spark
becoming the portrait of happiness

Woven Strong

Your love weaves

Strength into

The threads of

My soul

Tattoo

I want to embed the memory of us

On my skin like a tattoo

Feeling each pinprick of your touch

Like a spark in the dark

Dead of night where we lay

Against each other miles apart

Though neither of us have moved

Lack of intentional intimacy

Gave way to uncomfortable comfort

Our love the warm embrace of an oversized hoodie

Now threadbare and drafty

Worn of its welcome though a welcomed memory

Soon bound for the donation box

Easily tossed and forgotten

Unlike a tattoo that may fade but never forgets

The beauty of what once was remaining

Painted as a masterpiece

That says "I had this...once"

Part V

FOR THE LOVE OF ROMANCE

Mosaic

Shards of past heartbreaks

Pieced together with mortar

My love is a mosaic of experience

A kaleidoscope of perspective

That envelops you in color

Glossy and matte simultaneously

Painting our future in the present

Until we're a portrait of possibility

Hung amongst the great works of art

Love Compromises

---

priorities shift

meld between the two made one

love compromises

You and I...We

You came to us complete and open;

I came to us completely wary.

You invited me in and left the ball in my court;

I picked it up and ran, unsure of the goal.

You promised nothing, yet gave what was needed;

I promised to be open and gave all I had.

We learned to dance in the waves.

I am settled security;

You are endless striving.

I am quiet contemplation;

You are enigmatic action.

I am comfort unrelaxed;

You are fashion refined.

We exist in balanced wonder.

You create to the early bird's song;
I create once the world is fully alive.
You dream up ideas unfettered;
I write words tethered in possibility.
You hum the rhythm of our world;
I imagine the world we could build.
We push each other forward, destination unknown.

The Choice

---

if given the chance

to start over tomorrow

I'd choose you again

Chemistry

Chemistry isn't always magical
spontaneous combustion
of charged energies.
Sometimes it's subtle,
a hypothesis that conditions matter,
that initial sparks fizzle,
that love is an experiment
of finding the right combination—
passion and playfulness,
trust and understanding,
ambition and admiration,
stability and compromise,
until the two become

dissolved in a solution

of mutual appreciation,

compounded in shared values.

The state of the matter—

Solid, liquid, gas—

is irrelevant

once they're inseparable.

Wrapped

Every touch of your hand
is a ribbon around my flesh
holding me together
though I feel shattered

Every taste of your lips
a bandage to my wounds
healing the hurts
with promises of tomorrow

Your love makes me eternal
mummified intact and dignified

Complementary Souls

---

the ice in my soul

craves the fire in your heart beat

complementing needs

The Book She Needed

This wasn't the book she'd ordered
She'd been stuck in the self-help section,
thinking her life in need of fixing,
imagining that things would just be better
if she was someone, anyone else.

This wasn't the book she'd ordered.
She looked at life as a memoir
chronicling eventful times gone by
rather than a series of potential
windfalls along the way to the future.

This wasn't the book she'd ordered.
She'd wanted a fantasy ending

with beautiful sprayed edges
to sit on a shelf and never be read
for fear of creasing the spine

This wasn't the book she'd ordered.
She liked her romance hard and fast,
trailing on the edges of dark
where monsters live in human form,
covering pain in lustful imagination.

This wasn't the book she'd ordered
because she couldn't find words
to describe the way you changed
the story she had been writing
to one of complementary plotlines.
This wasn't the book she'd ordered,
but you gave her the book she needed.

Breathless

In laughter

In tears

I turn to you

Breathless

Balance

On days I'm barely
holding myself together,
you are a pillar of strength.

During rare moments
of stressful determination,
I stand your encourager.

When I'm questioning
my willingness to push through,
you're my stalwart supporter.

Through moments of trust,
we found creativity
in mutual affection.

Though we are different

in a myriad of ways,

we're a perfect mosaic.

As times get tougher

and life is full of choices,

I will still choose you daily.

Lucid

---

we belong

in daydreams

lucid and colorful

like sunrise along the shore

where everything

glimmers free

and happy

The Small Things

There is a small book,

a painfully small, self-help book

that tells us to not sweat

over the minutiae, the small stuff,

warning that it is all small,

all so unimportant.

Yet,

it is the small stuff

that makes me sweat,

that stirs my soul,

drawing my thoughts to you.

The way your lip quirks up

when my skin is cold

as if you needed an excuse

to pull me near.

The way you come home from work,

a kiss on your lips,

a story to tell,

a moment that is just ours.

The way you watch the game,

head thrown back,

purring in your sleep,

my head in your lap, book in hand.

Big Feelings

---

a tad, bit, or smidge

ways we describe big feelings

our own love language

Everything Changed

Did you feel the change?
The moment when
curiosity was piqued,
when interest turned,
to lustful desire
when passions smoldered
into intimate comfort?

I felt it
the moment when
our eyes met,
when you held my hand
to your lips,
when you asked for a kiss

in the moonlight.

Everything changed
the moment when
I became whole
in your arms.

We're a Pair

Us

Soft

Playful

Comfortable

A pair of

Unmatched

Socks

Lazy Days

I love those lazy days

Those days where it's just

You and me

My head in your lap

Your fingers in my hair

Lulling me to sleep

As we sway back and forth

Beneath the rustling leaves

Cocooned in our hammock

Built for two

Along the Edge of Clouds

Along the edge of clouds
My senses dance
The rhythm of romance
Along the edge of clouds

My senses dance
In time to your heartbeat
The graceful tapping of my feet
My senses dance

In time to your heartbeat
I syncopate my breaths
Inhaling to profound depths
In time to your heartbeat

I syncopate my breaths

Holding onto each moment

A touch of perfection present

I syncopate my breaths

Holding onto each moment

Captured by the smile in your eyes

As we move through the skies

Holding onto each moment

Captured by the smile in your eyes

Enticed by the curve of your lip

Daring to get drunk off one sip

Captured by the smile in your eyes

Along the edge of clouds

My senses dance

The rhythm of romance

Along the edge of clouds

Lying in Wait

Lying in bed

Dreaming a picturesque window

Waves lapping the shore

Cuddled in your arms

Waiting for the sun to shine

I Feel Your Music

I feel your music

In the way your notes

Syncopate like heartbeats

Chest to chest

I feel your music

In the rhythm

Of your fingertips

On my skin

I feel your music

In the way melodies

Rise and fall

From your lips

I feel your music

In the way chords

Tie us together

In distant harmonies

I feel your music

As a symphony

Of emotions

Rising to crescendo

Before descending

Into the smooth groove

Of calming waves

I feel your music

Content

I sing a cat's purr

sinewy smooth vibrations—

content in your arms

Part VI

FOR THE LOVE OF SELF

Yellow in a Desert Sea

Fertile ground produces

brilliant blooms,

but even the desert

sprouts spectacles.

Your roots go deep,

grounded in purpose.

Your stalks grow tall,

stable and strong.

Your leaves spread wide,

steeped in wisdom.

And like the Black-Eyed Susan

drowning in a sea of brown,

your petals solicit attention.

Matured and miraculous,

your very existence,

the verity of your thriving,

is the promise of perseverance

others only hope for.

Self-Love Reimagined

So many say,

"You can't pour

from an empty cup,"

but they don't see

the holes they

bore into the tin.

I say "Just wait

for the arrival of

Spring and see

how well you can

water your garden

through the holes."

Self-love,

Self-preservation,

Self-care,

isn't about looking

to make yourself

whole again but

in seeing beyond

the cracks.

Treat them gently,

fill them with gold,

show them off,

and stand tall

in the rubble

of all that tried

to break you.

Believe

Feel deeply

See clearly

Listen closely

Believe in

Your truth

Vine-Ripened

Running freely

Through

Seas of dreams

Flip-flopping

Cartwheeling

Untempered

Giggles flowing

Youthful lust

Naively immortal

Joie de vivre

Visible

As the luscious

Promise of

A juicy plum

Carefree

On the vine

Tethered

Yet free

To fall

Into maturity

If left alone

To ripen

Fully

Renovations

---

reformation time

shaped in clay molded by hand

silent permission

Crescendos of Affirmations

It went from hushed to roaring

The voice in my head

Telling me to break free

To let go of my chains

That kept me shackled to the past

The promise of a new day

Went from hushed to roaring

Like a babbling brook

Opening to a raging river

Refusing to be ignored

I opened my heart

And my voice

Went from hushed to roaring

Acknowledging obstacles

And all I have endured

Stepping into my own

Bringing forward my flaws

Like reopened scars

Went from hushed to roaring

Discovery of beauty marks

Long-forgotten dreams

Resurfaced from the quagmire

Where screams now

Echoed words of affirmation

That went from hushed to roaring

Eclipse

There is strength in holding on
But also strength in letting go
Releasing the bonds that
Have held you back until
You have healed enough
To eclipse the flames of fear
That shone bright beyond
Their years

In the darkening totality
Slip on the diamond ring
Of self-proclaimed love
And let your corona shine
Flushed with promenances

ECLIPSE

Where your sparks

Of brilliance invite

A nocturnal awakening

Of dreams improbable

Be no longer a beacon

Of nightmares

Hide no longer yourself

In shadows

Step into the light

And make your mark

On history

Follow the Author

Currently Available Books:

When Can We Be Soft?: Poems of Female Resilience

Lilli and the Nervous Narwhal

Follow Bobbie all over social media:
https://linktr.ee/bisabelwrites

See the website for the latest updates on her writing endeavors and a poetry blog. All of her books are available signed in the shop on the website:
https://bisabelwrites.com

<u>Coming Soon:</u>

Summer 2024: The Maenad—Age of the Forgotten Ones
Book One
A fantasy coming-of-age novel

www.ingramcontent.com/pod-product-compliance
Lightning Source LLC
Chambersburg PA
CBHW031445120626
46545CB00006B/2564